Over in the Jungle

A rain forest baby animal counting book

By Marianne Berkes

Illustrated by Jeanette Canyon

DAWN PUBLICATIONS
CONNECTING CHILDREN AND NATURE

Over in the jungle,
where the trees greet the sun,
lived a mother marmoset
and her marmoset **one**.

"Swing," said the mother.
"I swing," said the **one**.
So they swung and they hung
where the trees greet the sun.

1

Over in the jungle,
wearing wings of shiny blue,
lived a Morpho butterfly
and her little Morphos **two**.

"Flit," said the mother.
"We flit," said the **two**.
So they flitted and they fluttered,
wearing wings of shiny blue.

2

Over in the jungle,
on a leafy canopy,
lived a noisy mother parrot
and her little parrots **three**.

"Squawk," said the mother.
"We squawk," said the **three**.
So they squawked and they walked
an a leafy canopy.

3

Over in the jungle,
on a rain forest floor,
lived a leaf cutter ant
and her little ants **four**.

"Scurry," said the mother.
"We scurry," said the **four**.
So they scurried and they hurried
on a rain forest floor.

4

Over in the jungle,
near a big bee hive,
lived a mother honey bear
and her little honeys **five**.

"Scramble," said the mother.
"We scramble," said the **five**.
So they scrambled and they rambled
toward a big bee hive.

5

Over in the jungle,
curled around some mossy sticks,
lived a long mother boa
and her little boas **six**.

"Squeeze," said the mother.
"We squeeze," said the **six**.
So they squeezed and were pleased,
curled around some mossy sticks.

6

Over in the jungle,
in bromeliad heaven,
lived a poison dart frog
and her little froggies **seven**.

"Hop," said the mother.
"We hop," said the **seven**.
So they hopped and they plopped
in bromeliad heaven.

7

Over in the jungle,
where she knew how to wait,
lived a mother ocelot
and her ocelots **eight**.

"Pounce," said the mother.
"We pounce," said the **eight**.
So they pounced and they bounced
and they learned how to wait.

8

Over in the jungle,
hanging from a heavy vine,
lived a super-slow sloth
and her little sloths **nine**.

"Creep," said the mother.
"We creep," said the **nine**.
So they crept, then they slept,
hanging from a heavy vine.

9

Over in the jungle,
in their rain forest den,
lived a father howler monkey
and his little howlers **ten**.

"Hoot," said the father.
"We hoot," said the **ten**.
So they hooted and they hollered
in their rain forest den.

10

Over in the jungle, come on, let's take a peek!

In the busy rain forest, they're playing hide-and-seek.

"Find us," say the children, "from ten to one."

When you find all the creatures, then this rhyme is done.

10 howler monkeys

9 sloths

8 ocelots

7 poison dart frogs

6 boas

5 honey bears

4 leaf cutter ants

3 parrots

2 Morpho butterflies

1 marmoset

Over in the Jungle

Sung to the tune
"Over in the Meadow"

Traditional tune
Words by Marianne Berkes

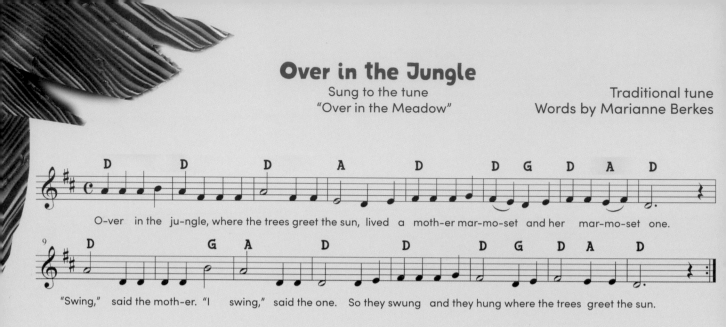

O-ver in the ju-ngle, where the trees greet the sun, lived a moth-er mar-mo-set and her mar-mo-set one.

"Swing," said the moth-er. "I swing," said the one. So they swung and they hung where the trees greet the sun.

2. Over in the jungle, wearing wings of shiny blue,
lived a Morpho butterfly and her little Morphos two.
"Flit," said the mother. "We flit," said the two.
So they flitted and they fluttered, wearing wings
of shiny blue.

3. Over in the jungle, on a leafy canopy,
lived a noisy mother parrot and her little parrots three.
"Squawk," said the mother. "We squawk," said the three.
So they squawked and they walked on a leafy canopy.

4. Over in the jungle, on a rain forest floor,
lived a leaf cutter ant and her little ants four.
"Scurry," said the mother. "We scurry," said the four.
So they scurried and they hurried on a rain forest floor.

5. Over in the jungle, near a big bee hive,
lived a mother honey bear and her little honeys five.
"Scramble," said the mother. "We scramble," said the five.
So they scrambled and they rambled toward a big bee hive.

6. Over in the jungle, curled around some mossy sticks,
lived a long mother boa and her little boas six.
"Squeeze," said the mother. "We squeeze," said the six.
So they squeezed and were pleased, curled around some
mossy sticks.

7. Over in the jungle, in bromeliad heaven,
lived a poison dart frog and her little froggies seven.
"Hop," said the mother. "We hop," said the seven.
So they hopped and they plopped in bromeliad heaven.

8. Over in the jungle, where she knew how to wait,
lived a mother ocelot and her ocelots eight.
"Pounce," said the mother. "We pounce," said the eight.
So they pounced and they bounced and they learned
how to wait.

9. Over in the jungle, hanging from a heavy vine,
lived a super-slow sloth and her little sloths nine.
"Creep," said the mother. "We creep," said the nine.
So they crept, then they slept, hanging from a heavy vine.

10. Over in the jungle, in their rain forest den,
lived a father howler monkey and his little howlers ten.
"Hoot," said the father. "We hoot," said the ten.
So they hooted and they hollered in their rain forest den.

11. Over in the jungle, come on, let's take a peek!
In the busy rain forest, they're playing hide-and-seek.
"Find us," say the children. "From ten to one."
When you find all the creatures, then this
rhyme is done.

Fact or Fiction?

The story in this book is based upon the popular song, "Over in the Meadow." In this variation, all the rain forest animals behave as they have been portrayed. That's a fact! But do they have the number of babies as in this rhyme? No, that is fiction.

Animal parents sometimes take care of their babies; sometimes they do not. The mammals in this story nurse their babies, and usually have either one baby (in the case of the honey bear, sloth, and howler monkey) or two (marmoset and ocelot). The mother parrot in this story lays two to four eggs and finds food for her babies after they hatch. The mother frog lays eggs which hatch into tiny tadpoles. She then moves the tadpoles into bromeliads for safety, and feeds them until they become frogs. (The bromeliad is a plant that may contain pools of water, acting as a habitat for many aquatic organisms! The most well know organism is a pineapple.)

The queen leaf cutter ant lays thousands of eggs in a nest, which she tends until enough worker ants have hatched to take over. Mother boas give birth to live young, usually twenty at a time, and the baby snakes fend for themselves immediately. Mother butterflies lay eggs and leave. The eggs develop into caterpillars, which later transform into butterflies. Nature has very different ways of ensuring the survival of different species.

The Rain Forest Community

Tropical rain forests are the richest forests on Earth. Even though these lush green forests cover only seven percent of the Earth's land, more than half the world's plants and animals live there. These exotic forests are found in a belt around the equator called the tropics.

There are four layers of tropical rain forest where these animals live. From bottom to top, they are:

Forest floor, which is covered with leaf litter, where fungi and insects thrive.
Understory, a darker environment, made up of smaller trees over the ground.
Canopy, which is filled with an incredible number of animals because of its thick leafy environment.
Emergents, where the tops of trees rise above the canopy as high as two hundred feet.

Tropical rain forests are so important that they are called the "lungs of the Earth." The trees in the rain forest release oxygen, which we need to breathe. If you want to learn more about this remarkable ecosystem and its creatures, go online to rainforest-alliance.org/programs/education, and be sure to check out the English/Spanish website of the Children's Eternal Rain Forest in Costa Rica, acmcr.org.

About the Animals

MARMOSETS are the smallest monkeys in the rain forest, only 7 to 12 inches tall. Their habitat is high up where they swing from tree to tree, grabbing food with their little claws. They eat spiders and other insects as well as fruits, bird's eggs, and lizards.

MORPHO BUTTERFLIES are brilliant blue with large wings that catch the light and make them shine. An adult Morpho flits from one fruit to another, drinking the nectar of rotting fruit with it straw-like proboscis.

PARROTS are noisy, intelligent birds that can always find food in the rain forest because their heavy hooked bills can scoop out fruit and crack seeds. Parrots fly together in pairs or small flocks and like to walk (and squawk) in the trees.

LEAF CUTTER ANTS are fascinating rain forest insects. They scurry around looking for leaves to cut and bring back to their underground colonies where they fertilize the leaves with saliva. This causes fungus to grow, which then serves as their food supply.

HONEY BEARS, also called kinkajous, have long prehensile tails that help them climb as they scramble clumsily around the canopy, looking for fruit, insects, and honey to eat. The furry kinkajou is known as the honey bear because one of its favorite foods, taken from the bees' nests, is honey!

BOA CONSTRICTORS are snakes that can grow up to 12 feet long. They live in the understory of the rain forest where they eat meat—rats, mice, lizards, fish, birds, and even wild pigs. When they are ready to strike, their fangs pop out and they squeeze their prey.

POISON DART FROG — There are many species of frogs in the rain forest, but the one chosen for this book is the poison dart frog, whose skin is so dangerous that native hunters use it to coat their hunting arrows. The female hops long distances to put her tadpole babies into a bromeliad high in the treetops for safety.

OCELOTS are medium-sized spotted cats of Central and South America. They look like small leopards and often stretch out on tree branches, spying on other animals. Graceful, fast hunters, they are most active at night, and pounce on their prey.

SLOTHS are slow-moving animals that creep around in the canopy. They have long, coarse fur that is so damp that moss and algae grow on it. This helps the sloth hide from its enemies. Sloths spend most of their lives hanging upside down, even when they sleep.

HOWLER MONKEYS are named for their loud, hooting calls, which can be heard up to three miles away. The male monkey's roar is the loudest and warns other monkeys to stay away from his territory where his group is living and feeding, mostly on leaves in the canopy.

Tips from the Author

I hope you will read my book often, each time discovering something new and exciting. A great reward, as a visiting children's author and storyteller, is to hear a child shout, "Read it again!"

Over in the Jungle offers many opportunities for extended activities. Here are a few ideas:

- In addition to counting the ten rain forest creatures, what other living things can you find and count?
- Use rain forest animal puppets and a rain stick as "story stretchers."
- Draw and cut out masks for each rain forest creature. Each child can act out the story with his or her mask.
- Talk about the different layers of the rain forest where the animals live and have the children create a rain forest diorama using polymer or modeling clay.

HERE IS A SPECIAL TREAT THAT I'VE WRITTEN FOR THIS BOOK!

As you sing or read the story, try using different body movements for each animal's action.

Marmoset swing: Swing right arm across body on the word "swing," then left arm on second "swing." (Arms are now crossed.) Raise them up high on "hung" and grab the air with your fingers.

Morpho flit: Slowly wave both arms at sides for "flit," then bring hands together in front and flutter fingers quickly.

Parrot squawk: Stamp right foot on first "squawk" and left foot on second "squawk." Then walk stiffly with tiny sideward steps.

Leaf cutter ant scurry: Get down on hands and feet and quickly scurry to the right and hurry to the left.

Honey bear scramble: With arms at sides, raise one shoulder to ear on "scramble" and then the other. On "scrambled and rambled", move both shoulders forward in a circular motion.

Boa constrictor squeeze: On the floor, curl on one side, stretching arms way out in front and pull in as if squeezing, on the words, "squeezed" and "pleased."

Poison dart frog hop: Hop on one foot, then the other, and quietly fall down on "plop."

Ocelot pounce: Bending forward, place hands under chin as if waiting. Then jump forward on first "pounce" and backward on second "pounce." Then jump up and down on "bounced."

Sloth creep: Get on back and move shoulders backwards slowly on "creep." On the word "slept," raise legs as if hanging and hold without moving.

Howler monkey hoot: Place one hand under armpit on first "hoot", and other hand under other armpit on second "hoot." Now flap both arms with hands still under armpits on "hoot and holler."

Tips from the Artist

The illustrations I make for my books are created with polymer clay. As a picture book artist and former early childhood arts educator, I believe that polymer clay is a wonderful, friendly, pliable and colorful medium for both children and adults to work with. As a fine artist, I love to create art with an array of colors, patterns and textures, and to make things with my hands—just as children do!

My studio is actually a lot like a kitchen. I store the clay in a refrigerator. (I should say "polymer clay" because it is not like clay dug from the earth, but is actually a non-toxic clay-like material.) I have an array of shaping tools including a pasta machine, food processors, cake decorating tools, and other utensils. And there's an oven in which the "pictures" are baked after they are all pieced together. The original art for the pictures in this book are not flat, which is very satisfying to me because it speaks to my love for both sculpting and painting. The art is called "relief sculpture": sculptures projecting from a flat surface. To create the two-dimensional illustrations you see in my books, the relief sculptures are photographed (with careful attention to lighting).

Polymer clay offers people of all ages unique ways to communicate and express ideas, as well as to experiment using textures, patterns, and colors. You will find many colors available in hobby and art stores—even some translucent and glow-in-the-dark colors. I encourage you to let your imagination soar while you have fun creating your own colorful clay "jungle friends!" I would love to see some of your own creations and hear what discoveries you have made.

There are many tools and machines I work with to create my pictures out of polymer clay. One of my favorite gadgets is my food processor. Look at the backgrounds of all of the pictures in this book—I made all of those little balls by tossing different colors of clay into my food processor.

It's fun to work with molds. Sometimes I create molds out of polymer clay and sometimes I mold my clay around objects to capture their shapes, patterns, and textures. For the butterflies in this book, I created their wings by molding very thin layers of clay over seashells.

I love sculpting with polymer clay. I use my fingers and lots of different sculpting tools to shape and form the subjects in my pictures. Here I am using small knitting needles to sculpt the face of one of the howler monkeys. Some of my sculpting tools are very tiny so I can create fine little details in places where my fingers are too big.

Research is often an important part of creating my art. I go to libraries, museums, and anyplace I can go to learn about the subject matter in my pictures. I also do a lot of research using my computer, but my favorite way to do research is going out in nature. Much of my research for this book was done by visiting a zoo and conservatory close to my home.

Marianne Berkes has spent much of her life as an early childhood educator, children's theater director, and children's librarian. She is the award-winning author of over twenty-three interactive picture books that make learning fun. Her books, inspired by her love of nature, open kids' eyes to the magic found in our natural world. Marianne hopes young children will want to read each book again and again, each time learning something new and exciting. Her website is MarianneBerkes.com.

Jeanette Canyon received her bachelor of fine arts degree from the Columbus College of Art & Design. Inspired by the philosophy and schools of Reggio Emilia, Italy, she enjoyed a distinguished career as an artist and arts educator of young children. She now spends her time creating art for children's books and visiting schools. She has illustrated two other books in polymer clay, *Over in the Ocean* and *City Beats*. Jeanette's husband, Christopher Canyon, is also a renowned children's book artist.

For Emily, Libby, Samantha, Jay, Christina and Will.
Also special thanks to my friend, movement specialist Jean McAdam,
for her ideas on the body movement section of this book. —MB

I dedicate this book to my grandparents: Navona Pagels and Erwin "Red" & Lenore Martens.
Thank you for your stories and your encouragement and support of my creative
endeavors (and letting me act like a monkey sometimes)! —JC

Text © 2007, 2021 by Marianne Berkes
Illustrations © 2007, 2021 by Jeanette Canyon
Original art photographed by Jeff Rose Photography, Inc.
Cover and internal design © 2021 by Sourcebooks
Series design by Kelley Lanuto

Published by Dawn Publications, an imprint of Sourcebooks eXplore
P.O. Box 4410, Naperville, Illinois 60567–4410
(630) 961-3900
sourcebookskids.com

Originally published in 2007 in the United States by Dawn Publications.

Library of Congress Cataloging-in-Publication Data is on file with the publisher.

Source of Production: Kingery Press, Effingham, IL, USA
Date of Production: June 2021
Run Number: 5022432

Printed and bound in the United States of America.
KP 10 9 8 7 6 5 4 3 2 1

ALSO BY MARIANNE BERKES AND DAWN PUBLICATIONS

Baby on Board: How Animal Parents Carry their Young — These are some of the clever ways animals carry their babies!

Over in the Ocean — With unique and outstanding style, this book portrays a vivid community of marine creatures.

Over in the Arctic — Another charming counting rhyme introduces creatures of the tundra.

Over in the Forest — Follow the tracks of forest animals, but watch out for the skunk!

Over in Australia — Australian animals are often unique, many with pouches for the babies. Such fun!

Over in a River — Beavers, manatees, and so many more animals help teach the geography and habitats of ten great North American rivers.

Over on a Mountain — Twenty cool animals, ten great mountain ranges, and seven continents, all in one story!

Over in the Grasslands — Come along on a safari! Lions, rhinos, and hippos introduce the African Savanna.

Over on the Farm — Welcome to the farm, where pigs roll, goats nibble, horses gallop, hens peck, and turkeys strut! Count, clap, and sing along.

Over on a Desert — Camels, tortoises, roadrunners, and jerboas help teach the habitat of the desert.

Going Around the Sun: Some Planetary Fun — Earth is part of a fascinating "family" of planets.

Going Home: The Mystery of Animal Migration — A book that is an introduction to animals that migrate.

Seashells by the Seashore — Kids discover, identify, and count twelve beautiful shells to give Grandma for her birthday.

The Swamp Where Gator Hides — Still as a log, only his watchful eyes can be seen.

What's in the Garden? — Good food doesn't begin on a store shelf in a box. It comes from a garden bursting with life!

OTHER NATURE BOOKS FROM DAWN PUBLICATIONS

Tall Tall Tree — Take a peek at some of the animals that make their home in a tall, tall tree—a magnificent coast redwood. Rhyming verses and a one-to-ten counting scheme made this a real page-turner.

Daytime Nighttime, All Through the Year — Delightful rhymes depict two animals for each month, one active during the day and one busy at night. See all the action!

Octopus Escapes Again! — Swim along with Octopus as she searches for food. Will she eat or be eaten? She outwits dangerous enemies by using a dazzling display of defenses.

Paddle, Perch, Climb: Bird Feet Are Neat — Become a bird detective as you meet the feet that help birds eat—so many different shapes, sizes, and ways to use them. It's time for lunch!

Dandelion Seed's Big Dream — A charming tale that follows a seed as it floats from the countryside to the city and encounters all sorts of obstacles and opportunities.

A Moon of My Own — An adventurous young girl journeys around the world accompanied by her faithful companion, the Moon. Wonder and beauty await you.